BABUSHKA'S BEADS:
A GEOGRAPHY OF GENES

Books and Chapbooks by the Author

GUY WIRES Poets' Choice Publishing (2015)

IN HASTE I WRITE YOU THIS NOTE: STORIES & HALF-STORIES
  Washington Writers' Publishing House (e-book 2015)

TIGER UPSTAIRS ON CONNECTICUT AVENUE
  Cherry Grove Collections, WordTech Communications (2013)

FEATHERS, OR, LOVE ON THE WING
  Shelden Studios, collaboration with artists Megan Richard, Suzanne Shelden
  (2013)

FROM THE ARTIST'S DEATHBED Winterhawk Press (chapbook 2012)

CORMORANT BEYOND THE COMPOST
  Cherry Grove Collections, WordTech Communications (2011)

REAL TOADS Black Buzzard Press (chapbook 2008)

AWAITING PERMISSION TO LAND
  Cherry Grove Collections, WordTech Communications (2006)

THE SPIRIT OF THE WALRUS Bright Hill Press (chapbook 2005)

IN HASTE I WRITE YOU THIS NOTE: STORIES & HALF-STORIES
  Washington Writers' Publishing House (2000)

THE ARC OF THE STORM Signal Books (1998)

ELEGY FOR THE OTHER WOMAN: NEW & SELECTED POEMS
  Signal Books (1996)

WILD GARLIC: THE JOURNAL OF MARIA X.
  Harper Collins (novella-in-verse, chapbook 1995)

A WOUND-UP CAT AND OTHER BEDTIME STORIES
  Palmerston Press (chapbook 1993)

FLYING TIME: STORIES & HALF-STORIES Signal Books (1986, 1988)

THE PROBLEM WITH EDEN
  Armstrong State College Press (chapbook 1985)

RAKING THE SNOW Washington Writers' Publishing House (1982)

A SHEATH OF DREAMS & OTHER GAMES Proteus Press (1976)

TIGHTENING THE CIRCLE OVER EEL COUNTRY
  Acropolis Books (1974)

TIMBOT The Lit Press (novella-in-verse, chapbook 1970)

Poetry Anthologies Edited:

THE DOLPHIN'S ARC: Poems on Endangered Creatures of the Sea SCOP (1986)

FINDING THE NAME The Wineberry Press (1983)

BABUSHKA'S BEADS:
A GEOGRAPHY OF GENES

New and Selected Poems

Elisavietta Ritchie

Poets' Choice Publishing

Foreword © 2016 Richard Harteis
Consultant work:
www.WilliamMeredithFoundation.org

Bulk discounts available through www.Poets-Choice.com

Cover artist: Sal d'Angelo
Author's photo: August Selk
Design consultant: Barbara Shaw

Library of Congress number pending
ISBN 978-0-9909257-9-8

Poets' Choice Publishing
337 Kitemaug Road
Uncasville, CT 06382
Poets-Choice.com

Elisavietta Giorgievna Hartmann Artamonoff and
Elspeth Cameron Ritchie

Acknowledgments

We thank the editors of the many individual publications where most of the poems in this collection first saw print, and the presses which reprinted them in the author's books for over four decades. A detailed list of the credits can be found at the end of this collection.

Special thanks to editor-publisher Richard Harteis, Jorge Nikolaevich Artamonoff, Eugenie de Shmidt Chavchavadze, David Pavlovich Chavchavadze, Lucy Obolensky Flam, Eli Flam, Suzanne F. Shelden, Craig Shelden, Annette Stewart, and especially to Clyde Henri Farnsworth. All have helped and encouraged the author for years.

We thank the photographers, most distinguished if long forgotten but for Louis Held, court photographer of the Weimar Republic, who photographed Eugenya von Lerche Erhardt as a girl, and the author, who photographed her children together, with their grandfather, and with their great-grandmother.

TABLE OF CONTENTS

Foreword

By Richard Harteis

It seems you can't get out of life without at some point needing to sit through a friend's slide show of their summer vacation, or listen to a garrulous cocktail hostess who feels she has to say everything that crosses her mind. It goes with the territory of being human. But Elisavietta Ritchie's rich autobiographical collection of poems only leaves you wanting more, not less.

Here is a woman who has really lived, and this verbal rumination on her heritage, the people she has loved, the family recipes for borscht or cherry vodka or bread, are filled with such exquisite, well-realized detail, a reader is drawn along with the force of a rip tide on a summer afternoon at the beach. It's all simply so interesting. And her conversations with the past and recently dead intrigue us: "It tolls for thee," they remind us, and yes, we all do eventually get out alive according to this wise woman when it comes our time to ponder the great mystery of death.

Russia's nostalgia for its glorious past – its literature, art, dance, theatre could not be extinguished in a century of Communist revisionism. This nostalgia seems worked into the very DNA of the Russian soul right down to the present day as the country seeks to take the world stage once again. At the root of this nostalgia is the ghost of a genteel aristocracy which ended in the forest assassination of the Czar's family and the Russian diaspora after the world wars that followed. As one of the world's great cultures, it continues to shape history and art and in this beautiful example, poetry.

Elisavietta Ritchie relishes her heritage and one may well ask what that heritage has to do with a new world democracy and a population set on assimilation and the future. For many young people today, history begins with their own personal life experience – past is not prolog, past is simply past. In a poem by William Meredith, he observes an old woman, a grandmother for whom the children open up like flowers because of her careful attention to them and their needs. "Perhaps that is why we are vouchsafed three generations," he says of the grandmother. "They are a teaching device."

And what we have to learn from the poems of Lisa Ritchie is everything worth preserving and protecting in life: Love, lovers, children, cousins, parents, home, shared meals, the memory of those who shaped us, the courage that won freedom, pride in self and country, an abiding attachment to the beloved dead reaching to us from the other side of life. Here are poems that extol life, sing of its joy, despite the cruelty and entropy that threaten at every turn. Lisa Ritchie is a person you would want to know, whose poetry you have here, life seen through her bright, intelligent, compassionate eyes, what poetry does at its best, give heart. An old proverb has it that "it is in the shelter of each other that we live." These poems give respite in a world too often in need of such shelter.

Because of an Old English Clock in Siberia: The Creation of This Collection

An unexpected request came from Bairma Bartanova, chief curator of Russia's only Clock Museum, in Angarsk, Irkutsk Oblast. She found me thanks to Michael Mints, a Russian historian who lived with us in Washington, 2012-2013.

"Our unique museum has a wonderful exhibit of an English clock from the late 18th-early 19th century. We knew almost nothing until recently about the previous owners, knew only that Maria L. Rickman, from Leningrad, donated the clock in 1976. Unfortunately, she did not tell how the clock came into her family.

"In April 2015 we received a letter from Natalia Alekseyevna Shemanova of Moscow. Her grandfather Vyacheslav Rickman and Maria Leonidovna's husband Vladimir/Volodya were first cousins. Natalya Alekseyevna gave a link to Michael Mints' website. And gradually, the picture began to emerge. Now it turns out that the clock was not made in England. There is a blot on the letters W. &. H. Sch. which refers to the German company Winterhalder & Hofmeier in the city of Schwarzenbach.

H.H. Schmidt's book *Lexikon der deutschen Uhrenindustrie 1850-1980* says that the firm of Winterhalder & Hofmeier produces high quality watches, some of the best clocks made in Germany. No wonder the trading house Pavel Bure chose it as one of its suppliers, along with the clock from the company Lenzkirch...On the mechanism of this clock, in addition to blot, there is an inscription made by hand in pencil: "1901 On 25 August Nikolsk" and an illegible signature.

"I beg you to talk about the parents of Mary Leonidovna and yourself. We know your grandfather, the Russian general, explorer and traveler Leonid K. Artamonov, was an outstanding individual. As for information about Elisavietta Hartmann Artamonoff, your grandmother, we have almost nothing. Few details about the brother of Maria Leonidovna, only initials, Yu. L. Artamonov: Yuri, probably, was this your father? We have many questions. We want answers..."

Bairma Bartanova's request inspired this collection wherein the poems tend to be more narrative than "poetic." My poems won't give the exact information she seeks, but something else about the individuals. Nor can I neglect others who played significant roles in my life...Certain princes, and Genghis Khan fifty-nine grandfathers back, may not need poems. Yet as I told my offspring:

> We check "Caucasian" for a reason:
> my father's ancestors came from
> the Caucasus: forbearers wed two
> genuine princesses, Tartar and Turk...

> ...We can all re-invent our pasts.
> You will manage your own and add
> whatever input you choose...

Are simple answers always simple for poets of Russian blood? Consider the seeming simplicity of Pushkin's poem:

> "I loved you once.
> Love may not entirely be
> Extinguished in my soul.
> Yet may this not disturb you anymore..."

I trust that all whom I loved, albeit now but snowy ghosts, are glad to be disturbed...

Elisavietta Yurievna Artamonoff Ritchie Farnsworth
January 2016

4

I

General Leonid Konstantinovich Artamonoff circa 1904

Novgorod Ikon

An angel, crimson robes and sharp black
wings, waves blessings to a horsy crowd
as saintly knights set off for war.

He's got a pile of bright celestial coins—
which side should he bet? At each
angelic ear a fluid personage advises:

"Bet that black horse!"
"The white mare's best!"
"The Lord is on *our* side!"

Both sides ask His patronage. Why God
should bless this battle, alone He knows.
Angelled sky and flowered field now gold,

sky and field and knights will soon be red,
the white mare nibbling grass,
black stallion with green knight, dead.

Then with emerald sleeves
and sharp black wings
the angel sweeps the winnings in.

In The Archives

In a long-dead English journalist's frayed
pages, scratchy maps and browned
photographs show half-baked campaigns:

soldiers defend the trenches with antique rifles,
visiting princes inspect wrecked cannons,
anonymous prisoners slog through towns
with unpronounceable names...

Look! My grandfather's photograph!
I never met my *Dedushka*...

My father described how his father explored
Abyssinia, Algeria, Central Asia, Siberia.
wrote books on his travels, commanded fortresses,
sailed to America to sign the Peace of Portsmouth,
NH, 1905, end of the Russo-Japanese War.

Back in Russia, he fought in more hopeless wars.

Here, as governor-general of captured Galicia,
he poses soldier-straight beside the Tsar's portrait.
For the camera he trimmed his moustache,
scraped the mud of battles from his boots,
and pinned the parade of medals on his chest.

Known as both "a walking encyclopaedia"
and a "brilliant fool on good terms with God,"
he won the love of his troops, envy of peers,
respect of the foe, and the gratitude
of emperors, prisoners, refugees.
He survived a court martial with honor.

But the year is 1915.
He will not govern for long.

Both sons will uphold the family name
on shifting battlefields.
Ivan will die fighting with valor,
Yuri will escape, and thrive in exile,
Maria will be forbidden to leave.

Despite wars, revolution, famine,
internal exile to distant cities to teach,
two terms in prison, lugged out for dead,
Dedushka won't abandon his damaged land.

His ruined heart will fail him.
Books recording his deeds will be lost
or banned, later revived, facts distorted.

Now, in a foreign journalist's book,
he still reviews his troops in the archives.

Gen. Leonid Konstantinovich Artamonoff flanked by the two Cossacks with whom he dodged crocodiles as they swam the Nile pushing a makeshift raft bearing the French flag to plant this on Egyptian soil because the Frenchman supposed to do this was ill with fever so remained behind in Ethiopia.

Orders to a Scribe

We stand a dagger's length apart—
You insist I chronicle his life.
I switch on the tape recorder in my skull…

> A Circassian prince, rigid, tall and spare,
> your slanted mountain eyes, black knives,
> slash me with their dark tenderness across
> the music of chunguris, tambourines, guitars.
> Your lizard swiftness splits me when you leap
> to dance lezghinkas, kinjal in your teeth.

I float around you, conscious of my décolletage.
A tape recorder winds, unwinds,
from reel to reel to reel beneath my ribs…

> Suddenly I am afraid you are entangling me…
> But who will dare record
> our dangerous entanglement—

Shared Ancestors

*"I see them, I talk to them, understand them through
the blank spaces left between words, in their letters,
and they are all in me." Jorge Nicholaevich Artamonoff*

They visit me too, dearest cousin,
though I am still loath to cross
that abyss into sparse stratosphere
where *they* wait for us.

Hands stretched in welcome,
they promise to answer our questions,
open their airy archives,
fill blanks in dusty dossiers.

Already their fingernails fracture
our windowpanes, sketch red
trails on our skin, write in blood
they remind is our own—

Enough that *your* blood
pounds through my veins,
we speak between words.
Please pull us back from the edge.

Georgi Hartmann, Privy Counselor,
Father of Elisavietta Georgievna Hartmann Artamonoff

The Ancestors Wait, Wet

in the chilly garage
across fields drenched
from days of rain

have waited years
in wooden trunks
keys lost

they persist in manuscripts
blue composition books
purple ink blurred

schoolboy essays on antique monarchs
tsars who tried to transform their lands
outlived their wars or not

letters written for fathers, sisters, progeny
for lovers locked in a soggy box
and careless descendants

who could not predict
the height of floods
the rage of hurricanes or wars

Abdication

Perhaps we can't outlive our palace:
We handed in our crowns,
they shut the gates.

Two deposed monarchs who too briefly ruled
an airy empire inside marble walls,
we governed only space, not time.

Elisavietta Georgievna Hartmann Artamonoff

Maria Leoniovna Artamonoff age 15
Elisavietta Georgievna Hartmann Artamonoff
Baroness Olga von der Osten-Sacken Hartmann

Leonid Konstantinovich and Elisavietta Giorgievna Artamonoff in Algeria

II

Babushka in America, 1933

Yuri purchased his mother's exit from the USSR.

After 15 dangerous years under Bolsheviks, NKVD,
the betrayal and disappearance of thousands of souls,
Famine Years when the Bolsheviks forced peasants
into collectives, harvests fell, and people starved,

she reached Ellis Island thin as an icon and terrified
censors here opened letters, every phone was bugged,
always one dinner guest was the informer. *But which?*

Best we all watch our words: any cop on the block
could send us all to the gulag—

Yet now she heaped sugar into her coffee,
raspberry jam in tea, honey on cottage cheese,
and oh, those cherries in chocolate!

And my father found an Armenian market
the far side of Chicago, bought home halvah.
She gained pounds but weight was okay.
I understood her desperation for sweets,
only slowly fathomed her fear to make plans:

"We might attend that concert next month *if*
I am still alive—" She had seen too many dead,
both sons were shot, one survived but in exile,
then her daughter was caught in the Blockade
and no way to learn if she were alive...

Teatime with Babushka, Age Ninety-Four

She describes how she put the Tsarina at ease
at Kronstadt Fortress with kind English words,

recalls the splendid count on Nevsky Prospekt
encountered years later in rags, who remembered
the lapis lazuli in her chestnut curls.

She agrees Rasputin was opportunistic and odd
but not, surely, as bad as Saint Petersburg hissed,
for though a nation's fate should outweigh a mother's love
that, too, was understandable.

She tells of the Bolshevik jail:
shoved into the prostitutes' cell,
she resolved their fights
and they begged her to stay in *their* cell,
not be moved to the aristocrats' wing.

She drinks her tea, grasps her cane,
pulls herself up, as always complains
old age is no joy, high time she died.

She kisses her great-grandson's hands
full of jellybeans, and leaves, discussing
Vietnam with the cabbie and God,

unaware this gray plastic comb
dropped from her hair.

Guest of Honor

She has visited me several times.
Not during the year right after she died
while buying her ticket to spend
one more birthday with us. Tonight.

Did she pass this last year in limbo?
Is it easier now to obtain her brief leave
as a novice gains nunship
and with it, a limited freedom?

She appears at our door with her same cry of joy.
I help her over the threshold, take her coat,
foulard scarf and black cane. She smooths
her milkweed hair blown by an unknown wind.

The dining room laced with crepe paper streamers,
"Happy Birthday!" we shout. "Surprise!"
We speak loudly because she is deaf.
She joins in the singing, praises each gift,

blows out candles, licks icing off her stiff fingers,
winks at a child whose face I can't see,
and asks, "Whose birthday comes next?"
She crochets months ahead, just in case.

Oh! Babushka's vanished!
Cake crumbs, dabs of icing,
scraps of bright wrapping paper,
litter the table still…

Elisavietta Georgievna Hartmann Artamonoff circa 1960

Babushka's Beads

My grandmother pops up online and disappears
like diving ducks but not sharp black-and-white.
All gray: face, hair, lace collar. Loops of china beads
gleam white, marble-size, worn in place of pearls.

A long-lost cousin in Brazil emailed her photograph.
When and how did *he* obtain this formal shot?
How did she join my screensaver of passing images?

Dasha from Moscow glimpses Babushka online:
"*Inteligentnaya—means more than wise: such eyes see the soul.*"
Visual powers only Russians are allowed?

She segues past my eyes, a ghost too quick to print.
Then the screen goes dark.

Dates and strands remain uncertain as her life.
Sent to the Sorbonne at 16, she'd escape from lectures,
browse the stalls with books and paintings by the Seine.

Did a secret love give her the china beads?

Or were these a proper present from a future general?
Their marriage in St. Petersburg, 1899, the Tsarina came.

Distant postings, wars, revolutions, children lost,
famine, terrors, jails, haven in America, more wars…

By then our unstrung fates had intertwined.
I walked her paths beside the Hudson, Neva, Seine.

They sent me to the Sorbonne too. "Avoid French men,"
she warned. "Despite their gifts, they climb all over you."

Years slide past. She treasured those plain beads
more than sparkling gems, passed them on to me.

III

A young woman who served as wet nurse for the firstborn baby Ivan Leonidovich Artamonoff while nursing her own child on her other breast. She lived in a village within Troitskoye. As "milk brothers" the boys grew up closest friends, soon joined by Yuri and the other village children.

Family Ghosts

At16, Elisavietta Hartmann inherited a cousin's estate:
Troitskoye with three villages, a stone manor house, church,
and fertile land by a river south of Moscow, Tula Oblast.

The deed of transfer signed, family and lawyer went to bed.
Down in the study, the new owner bolted shutters and door
and slept on a couch, her two borzois across the threshold.

Midnight she woke screaming, "An old man! Blood-soaked
clothes of another century! In this locked room!" Everyone
rushed to help, servants smashed her door. The man was gone.

The elder villagers told the story: a century ago an early landlord,
cruel to his serfs, beat one to death. The judge levied mere fines
for landed gentry. The landlord paid and his troika headed home

through the birches and pines. Peasant women ambushed him,
beat him bloody with flails. He died in that room, his ghost
appears to each new heir. This time he visited you…

***

The wet nurse holding the baby Ivan, suddenly dropped him
and screamed, "The old man is here!" As if she, not Ivan
the first-born son and rightful heir, would inherit Troitskoye.

With the Revolution, the family fled to a Petersburg flat.
The villagers cared for it in case the former owners returned.
Troitskoye became a collective, the manor a Workers' club.

World War Two: the Red Army staff set up headquarters
in the manor. The Germans seized it, then again the Reds.
Did the ghost visit them, or know they were only in transit?

***

In the White Army retreat, Yuri, delirious from typhoid, a bullet through his leg,
slept on straw in a monastery near Kharkov.
Ivan appeared in his dream, said: "I was killed on the battlefield
but Yuri, you will live, go to a land where English is spoken."

The monolingual American doctor overheard Yuri speaking
English in his sleep, sped his recovery. They retreated, retreated,
in Crimea caught the last US Navy ship to leave Sebastopol.

***

After World War Two, in our brownstone house, 92nd Street,
Yuri, now George and American, was often the last in the den,
when the ghost (of a former owner?) walked up the stairs.

Snuffy, my auburn spaniel, watched every step and growled.
My mother, although herself clairvoyant, laughed
at my father's tales to entertain children and guests…

I was alone downstairs when Snuffy watched the ghost climb
four flights to my attic room. Awake or asleep, I never saw him.
But I did not own the house in Manhattan…

***

We learned the manor burned down. Visiting Russia in 1986,
I located Troitskoye but, beyond the neglected orchard,
found only tumbled stones. I did not spend the night.

My father, 84, sat up in the hospital bed across the Potomac.
"Lt. Ivan Leonidovich reported for duty this morning, saluted…
Our departed return near the time they must welcome us…"

***

Every year or so, another relative dies, far away. No chance
for farewells. Babushka visited once long ago. Neither parents
nor long-ago loves reappear though they still haunt my pages.

They are awaiting their turn. But I am not up for their visits.

Visiting Rites

The dead watch over those left here,
you assure me by my father's grave.
I've learned: it takes one year
till they return to us.

Perhaps they do need time
to pull away, learn solitude,
come to terms with their condition
while we here face our own.

We change the room, sort files,
distribute coats we cannot bear to see
hang empty, and hope not to know
who wears those shoes donated to a thrift.

They no longer need their clothes although
when they return, it's fully shod and clad
while we lie naked in our lonely sleep.
Yet we arise quite dressed, and offer them

a cup of tea, or wine, cherries, cake,
all somehow waiting on the table here.
We set the table every night in case
our long-absent husband, lover, son,

might walk in at last...I receive *your* visit,
in full knowledge in my dream:
you are a ghost, and slightly frightening,
and with dawn you will leave again.

Ivan Leonidovich Artamonoff, Yuri Leonidovich Artamonoff
Maria Leonidovna Artamonoff

Artamonoff family picnic including the governess Miss Gossett, cousins and friends by the Baltic, Elisavietta Giorgievna Hartman Artamonoff among the three ladies standing in the last row, Yuri Leonidvich Artamonoff and Maria Leonidovna Artamonoff in the front row, and Ivan Leonidovich Artamonoff standing apart.

The Odd One:

On seeing a photo of Teilhard de Chardin en famille

In those old photos,
family arranged like statues,
you may note one child
who stands apart with a solemn face,
stares in a different direction.

That one will go off,
never return.

Perhaps one daughter
won't look at the camera
takes to the road.

She may try to peddle her words
on the street, the sounds
of a clarinet, or a canvas
preserving familial blood
in smudged fingerprints,
but neglects postcards home.

Or like my uncle Ivan,
in a sepia photograph:
"*La famille en pique-nique,
aupres du Baltic 1911,*"
who filled student notebooks
with passionate novels,
before he went off to war,
was shot to death at nineteen.

Often they gave everything away.
If they were to come home,
hands empty, scarred,
try to fit themselves back

inside the frame among siblings
and nephews and nieces,

their eyes would glow
with prodigious visions –
char the paper,
splinter the frame,
smash the glass–

The Persistence of Uncle Ivan: 1900-1919

In boyhood photographs, Ivan's narrow face
is grave, his eyes dead serious, as if they knew.

In the Civil War between White and Red armies,
his novel written at 19 left unfinished in Leningrad
with his poems and schoolboy themes in purple ink,

he was shot in battle north of Kharkov near Putivl,
a hamlet not on my old map. Those who survived
described his courage: "he was tireless under fire."

Did his comrades bear his body to a church?
Find a priest to sing his soul to God?

Or, ever in retreat, did they leave him in a ditch,
scarce time to shovel that black earth, sign a cross?
Or just grab his rifle, fight, retreat, retrench, retreat…

Ivan invades my work, not yet my dreams.
Will we recognize each other then?
Am I answerable to him for my own poems
and novels left undone?

Wars pass, and years. In a visit to Russia, I search:
Is Ivan here in this potato field? Those woods
where later Nazis built their bunkers?

Or only in my imperfect words…
But I wait for him…

IV

Col. George/Yuri Leonidovich Artamonoff circa 1945

Like a Twin, If Ten Months Younger

In childhood photographs Yuri's face is round,
he smiles as if he could predict *he* would outlive
his wounds, leap aboard the last ship from Crimea—

In the Early Days of World War Two

My father beams in the photo from England.
Behind him, trees, and a church tower, squared—
the spire, I imagine, must be bombed off:

Even age eight, an ocean away, I read newspapers,
learn he will soon move on to the front,
his fine uniform become dusty, bloody, torn.

                    ***

Age 19 I visit an exquisite English lady
among her beds of rosemary, savory, lavender
all drawing ten species of bees.

On her bureau stands the duplicate photo
of the black-and-white snapshot on mine.
"I used up my last film on him," she sighs.

Her husband off in India, Malaya, Burma,
she billeted officers in her house
where she had plenty of space.

"And," he later tells me but not my mother,
"sympathy." He smiles over his memories.
I did not know to judge then, won't now.

My Father's *Vishnyovka*

"The demijohn must be glass, not a crock,"
he said. "Layer cherries and sugar, fill the jar.

Then cover with vodka, one hundred proof."
"Don't make it too strong!" Babushka argued.

He tied a cloth over the top to keep out bugs
and hauled the demijohn to the roof to get

as much sun as it would give. "Do not disturb
between cherry-picking time and the autumn!

Watch the liquid turn redder. Then pour it into
clean bottles, no need to distill. Dump the old fruit."

Babushka "didn't drink," except for a nightcap
of sherry or port "*doux et pas fort.*" So every day

she climbed the rickety stairs to the roof to check,
and all that summer seemed especially cheerful.

When the cherries were bled, she said, "Ready."
The liquid level had dropped. By evaporation?

The chickens discovered the discarded cherries,
staggered all day through the barnyard.

"In Florida now," Daddy writes, "we use local produce.
You should try your Babushka's latest *kumquatka!*"

My Father, Colonel, U.S. Army, Retired

The shell explodes and scatters light
and alien finger bones. He isn't sure
if this is real or dream
but screams until he wakes.

The household wakens, terrified.
He is embarrassed, and confused,
trapped back at Kharkov, Sebastopol,
Anzio, Monte Cassino, Normandy,
Germany, the Battle of the Bulge.

Forty years have passed, wars have not.
Shrapnel, rubble and peculiar shards of flesh
still litter all the bedroom floor so deep
he cannot find his slippers in the dark.

Improvements

My Dad can walk again! His mind as well
meanders streets he hasn't seen for years
as he renews his friendships with the dead.

He asks about my alimony and
how do I like my new koala bear
he brought from Australia 30 years ago.

He redirects the Battle of the Bulge, rewrites
Tannenberg, confers with Genghis Khan,
instructs his broker sell his Edsel fast.

We shuttle centuries and shuffle names.
I sing old songs, and try to make him taste
fake-grape Jello, bouillon and white bread.

He wants retsina, caviar, turtle eggs, insists
he must get dressed now to receive the Queen
of Belgium, some princess from Cleves.

Till they arrive, we'll stroll the corridor
from bed to chair, set four cups in a row,
boil tea, then deal out double solitaire.

Flying Time

"He asked me to fly to Bangkok with him,"
giggles the nurse. I picture my father's
wheel chair sprout aluminum wings,
his skeletal shoulders grow feathers–
scarlet, vermilion, green–
like a swan sired by a parrot.

"I hope you agreed to fly with him,"
I answer. "He was a famous explorer."

She laughs, slaps her plump palms
against her white uniform.
"Lord, what a spaced-out
i-mag-in-a-tion your daddy's got!"

His blue eyes watch us. I smooth
wisps of hair like down on his skull.
My mad daddy...

            Here are the springs
of my i-mag-in-a-tion...
At eighty-four may I too
have license for madness.

Meanwhile I wheel his chair
to his place at the table
between old Mrs. Silverman
screaming "Sugar! Coffee! More milk—"
and Muggsy sloshing soup on his neighbor.

I set the brakes, fasten his seat belt.
Although my father insists this trip
he would prefer smoked eel and vodka
then lamb curry and Indian beer,

I spoon pureed liver and unsalted limas
into his mouth quickly before
his fingers explore the plate.

Downstairs in the Ladies Room,
by mistake I enter the oversized stall
marked blue-and-white HANDICAPPED.
Handrails and a high commode.

But will there be space enough here
for my wings?

While Our Fathers Are Dying

We are reading to them. From the Bible,
from books they once read or wrote,
Dostoyevsky, Plato, our own—
anything, while we sit by the silent bed.

We believe a familiar voice
whether or not they respond
will snare them in our nets,
or give part of ourselves to take along
though they must now travel light.

Yesterday's paper keeps us up
with the world even as they pull out.
Yet they may hang on, not just
for the sound of our words.

We drone on. If they hear,
they know they are still alive.
Afterwards we continue to read aloud…

Now my father can no longer hear.
His cinders fill a hole beneath a cross
of stone big enough to keep him there
until I near *my* death:

that's the time when family ghosts appear
as Ivan visited his brother, mother, sister,
each in turn before they died...

While It Rains

The land swells,
puddles become lakes,
rivulets streams,
and inside the white room
my father shrinks,
bones hollow as birds'.

In our drowned garden
asparagus tips
spear spongy earth,
stretch toward the wet sky,
feather into wings
of emerald lace.

The largest limb
of the old locust tree
riddled by woodpecker beaks
crashes across the inlet,
sinks into the marsh.

Elbows and knees
fold up and close
like the dull blades
of his pocket knife.

When the river overflows,
bearing locust blossoms,
even whole oaks
toward the bay,
he floats away
light as a gull.

Root Soup, Boxing Day

"Each guest is sent to us by God—"
an old Caucasian song my father sang

We test the scumming broth
of last night's turkey bones.
The soup cries out for roots!
Turnips, parsnips, clumsy rutabagas!

       That Saturday I cleared out stones,
       planted seeds, buried in one final row
       cubed potatoes rife with sprouts.
       Then the phone: "Your father passed."

Tonight I mince the winter's parsley,
garlic, onions, cabbage, bay leaves
from the Christmas wreath,
worry will this be enough…

       My father told me how a soldier,
       young and hungry, asked for shelter
       in a peasant woman's hut.
       "But I have no food," she said.

       The soldier took a pebble from his pack,
       dropped it in her pot. Soon their soup
       steamed with unearthed miracles of roots,
       one strayed hen. They ate all week.

Now Ann arrives with carrots, Clyde with two
potatoes, Sergei—*beets*, and calls it borscht.
Our cauldron simmers as in my father's house…
He must have willed a stone to me.

A Geography of Genes

My father taught me to decode
wiggling lines and whorls
of valleys, buttes, deserts, coasts,
and their skewed-mirror images
on the ocean floor.

He showed me where Atlantis
might have floated,
the jigsaw puzzle of Gondwanaland,
how to locate North—
inconstant at the Pole.

My mother always found a beach
by scent of bayberry and salt.

His poor sense of direction
tugged him off course
yet he read flat clues
to rivers, hills and streets,

and in three dimensions
his fingertips deciphered
contours of his mistresses,
mapped journeys
of affection, infidelity....

Our tangled strands persist…
My compass needle's bent.
Stars remain illegible,
trails spiral, switchback up
mountains to the brink of cliffs.
My fingers learn to chart
risky landscapes in the dark,
slippery topographies,
the trickster North Pole shifts,
dangerous terrain, dead ends.

Now one lover claims he found
Atlantis sunken under water
southwest of Gibraltar.

I too would sound new latitudes,
set sail for the antipodes—

I tack along my father's routes,
lace a wavering geography
through icebergs, hurricanes,
the deadly calm Sargasso Sea,
constellations enigmatic, horizon fogged.

Yet with my mother's certitude
threads strong as hawsers pull me
to Gondwanaland, now split apart.
I redraw old maps, chart new lands,
then, path and port unsure, set off again.

IV

Maria Leonidovich Artamonoff Rickman
Vladimir/Volodya Rickman

Her Final Child

My Aunt Maria whom I'd never met, remained
in Leningrad, forbidden to follow her mother out:
she and Volodya must stay to build the New Russia.

Rare letters bore the censor's ink. She could send
children's books with poems so I'd learn Russian.
More wars cut all connections. Did she survive?

1986: I traced her to Pesochniye, a village on few maps
in that land of dangers, spies, arrests. Half-blind, still
she'd know me by the beads someday I'd leave for her.

Halvah, Toronto

To honor Babushka and Aunt Maria
I eat this Turkish concoction discovered
the far side of town: sesame seeds, nuts,
honey, mysterious spices, who knows which…

1986: I pack vitamins, Oreos, Belgian cakes, Swiss
chocolate bars, French pastries, but found no halvah…
In a distant village where barracks were houses
at last I find my elderly aunt sweeping the path…

Aunt Maria Leonidovna Tells War Stories

You brought sugar for our tea!

…Yes, dear, I wanted children but
the doctor botched my operation…
I adopted an orphaned cousin.
In the Siege she died of starvation…

The Nazis knew we were moving out
Leningrad's children by sleighs across
frozen Lake Ladoga, a highway of ice.
No amnesty: the Nazis strafed and shelled.

Inside the city, we preferred bombs:
loud whistles while dropping gave the alert
to rush to a shelter, and warned me:
climb to the artillery post on the roof.

But shells struck without warning—
suddenly someone fell at our feet.
We learned to step over corpses.
Hard to dig graves in the permafrost.

What good all my shiny medals
for bravery and survival?
You take the lot home.
Ah, the samovar remains warm.

Do have another cup—

Snow in Leningrad

1.

2002. Blizzard, Washington, I'm shoveling snow. My mind
sifts snow in Leningrad, World War Two, the Siege: I try
to track my Aunt Maria as she steps over snowy ruins and

humans felled by famine, illness, shells. Early dusk and snow
mask the dead, a while. No burials till the hard ground thaws.
She lugs rubble from wrecked buildings to raise new barracks.

Nights, she mans an anti-aircraft gun. One slice of bread a day.
Bombs hit her flat, in Pushkin's former stables. Volodya sends
his captain to find her. "Come, teach English to my officers:

someday they'll need it." At headquarters, with bread she gets
a cup of soup, a place to sleep, safer if not warm. But no one is.
Medals afterwards. She survives more famines, blizzards, visits

from the KGB. They allow her to teach English, French, keep
her piano, and when Volodya, still shrapnel in his skull, returns,
move to barracks Nazi prisoners built in a village to the north.

2.

1986. A luminous June. I dare not warn that we might meet.
As if expecting me, she serves tea, talks of skating on the Neva,
troika rides across Petersburg, walks with Akhmatova and Blok,

the 900 nights the Nazis ringed her wounded town, starvation.
Her champion Airedale vanished into someone's cooking pot.
Now a small white mutt and large gray cat sleep on her feet:

"Trust creatures more than certain humans…" Neighbors curious,
nervous, may have to report on strangers. But her friend Ludmila
is faithful, discreet, though the son may be reporting my visit…

3.

1991. Ludmila writes: *The ambulance sped your aunt across the Neva to hospital in Leningrad. Midnights she wakes the ward with her lectures on Pushkin, Dickens, Shakespeare and Voltaire.* I pack my bags.

My plane arrives at Sheremetyevo a day too late. By three metros and a bus as Ludmila leads me through the city deep in sooty snow. Not neighborhoods for foreigners. We skirt

the hospital on icy paths. *MORGUE.* A white-smocked man sweeps out a dappled cat who slips back in, resumes his watch beside a certain slab where my chilled aunt reclines in state.

She wears her blue professor dress, beret she said she would wear to her grave...Old students, fellow teachers, many friends. Through falling snow, we escort her to a marble crematorium.

The Church forbids it but the government is practical. Speeches almost like a service. The coffin slides through low brass doors. Attendants, thrifty, keep the clothes. Someone takes the ashes.

Mourners troop along Moika Canal to her old flat, repaired. We toast her soul's cold journey through the snowy skies. Come spring, ashes will go beneath a churchyard stone.

I would wear the china beads again, but Ludmila keeps them as her memento "since Maria left no heirs." Nor did Ludmila, but someday her son's new wife might like the pretty things.

4.

2002. Washington. In this wind swirling white
I seek Maria still...Still the night is blind. I try to fix her life
in words...Words freeze, then melt like flakes of snow.

As if these were the drifts that cloak
the stone above her distant sack of ash,
I keep on shoveling.

V

Eugenya von Lerche Erhardt

Thanksgiving with Great Aunt Eugenya

In daylight her mostly blind eyes could still see
bright colors and shapes, so my salad gleamed
with red pepper, yellow squash, green beans.

She lifted the silver fork over the gold-rimmed
Limoges plate, inspected it closely, recalled
a glistening bullet cut from the gangrenous leg

of a soldier. The doctor killed, she'd learned
to amputate on the battlefield. World War One, no
eligible men in town, young ladies became nurses.

No man in my house, and I was unsure how
to carve a turkey. Her fingers skilled in the Braille
of bones, the shining skin and the flesh stayed intact.

Hungry for history and science, my daughter and I
asked questions. Aunt Eugenya told of the family
estate by the Baltic, the last ball in St. Petersburg…

After the Revolution, Bolsheviks seized the estate,
made her work as a prison camp nurse. She signed
sick inmates to hospital: more food, chance to escape.

She too fled, to Estonia, a farm by a lake. Then
under Nazi rifles she managed a farm in Poland.
She shared her rations with *Ostarbeiter*, slave labor,

and shared their work: led horses, steered the plough,
planted, dug potatoes by hand. A buxom young lady,
she married a kindly German orchestra conductor.

The Nazis fled before the advancing Red Army. She
hitched up the horses, piled refugees in a cart, trekked
West, caught a boat to England, ran a boarding house...

In a Washington flat well-furnished with hand-me-downs
she treasured her tin army cup more than Willowware,
and worked again as a nurse as long as she still could see.

Born in a safer land and time, I bear the weight of
suffering only a small war first-hand...Best I can do
is hear out, absorb others' lives, try to nurture them...

My daughter became a doctor, learned war:
Cyprus, Lebanon, Korea, Somalia, Iraq at bad times.
C-rations from a pack on Thanksgiving.

Tonight we do not recite grace, but in silence thank
God for rainbows of food, a safe house, each other,
and for this interim peace.

Visiting Great Aunt Eugenya
Beside the Patuxent River

Each Spring, I visit her under the spruce
six yards from the water, yank pokeweed,
prune berry briars, but must not disturb
the cardinals' nest with four eggs.

Last April her nearly blind eyes still
distinguished the blaze of azaleas.
As always she expressed her surprise
she made it through one more winter.

She dictated her will while we sipped
my blackberry wine from jelly glasses:
"Make sure they burn my remains. Cast
my ashes onto a garden...Also into the sea."

We drank to her ninety-first year.
How fiercely her fingers gripped mine
that May afternoon as the strange
dry gargle churned in her throat.

I'd rented a farm by the water, dug in.
Now we dragged the canoe to the sickle
of beach, scattered half of her off the spit
of island where tides run strong.

Then after I'd cut back the weeds
I took the trowel, dug in the rest
beneath the spruce which stands alone
at the edge of the farmer's field.

His combine roars past like a tank
as he harvests wheat, soy beans and corn,

the last row so close he grazes the boughs
unaware she's here in his sandy soil.

I imagine her fragmented heart
is nourishing this singular spruce,
while blackberries burst from her bones,
chanterelles from her skull.

May she be reassured that part of herself
is planted in *terra firma* although
another portion will travel forever,
flutterkicking through foreign waves....

***

I must move on. The farmer ploughs
my asparagus under. Will he clear
the pokeweed, honeysuckle and briars
before they entangle her spruce?

Great Aunt Eugenya's Mattress

By then light as ash, her bones
barely shadowed the X-rays,
rest shrunken, no longer functional,
barely denting this mattress
now leaned against my garage.

Lumpy, narrow and thin.
No plasticized lavender patterns,
practical navy-striped canvas
with knobby buttons to hold
the cotton stuffing in place
till mice gnawed their way in.

A sepia snapshot shows her
buxom, flirtatious beside
the jovial conductor she married
before his orchestra folded
and he died at the front.

They'd not have both fit
on this skimpy mattress
but may they have enjoyed
full feather beds…

I must put this mattress out
as they put her out
in her tattered gown
for the funeral home limousine…

Navigating a New-Found Night

"In time, I'll go blind"
line from a last-year's poem

"I will miss the moon most of all—"
Through the cobwebs veiling her east-facing
windows and her eyes, Great Aunt Eugenya
could still make out the life of the sky.

"Please, Aunt Jenny, let me sweep and dust—"
"Thank you, no…Guests displace everything.
I know where *I* have put every object."
So she never let anyone clean…

I ordered her history Books-for-the-Blind.
Their reader recorded my own collection,
not wanting the author's voice.
Someday voice may be all I have…

En route to the hospital, she asked if the horses
were well hitched to our wagon, and she praised
the magenta azaleas, purple wisteria vines,
pink cherry trees, "this loveliest ever spring…"

    In time I too may go blind.
    This year might be the time:
    murky eyes, skull top-right
    in ungainly pain when I read.

    Never headaches before,
    mere aches of the heart
    for some lover vanished
    as her beloved did, years ago.

Were one of mine to return, would
I recognize him, make out whom
a mischievous fate has garbed
in clown suit, tuxedo or shroud?

I clear her flat, heap piles for friends, Goodwill, trash...
When *my* horses unhitch, my dust will be thick.
For now, I cherish books, azaleas, lovers, dust...
I too will miss the moon most of all...

VII

Sisterhood

On discovering a photo of the dusky girl
my father long described as his "old Moroccan
housekeeper," and learning they had a baby

Might my half-sister survive beneath the palms
of Marrakesh? Our father told me—not my mother—
of his lovely Moorish housekeeper early in the war.
Her photo tumbled from his tattered address book.

Although the housekeeper surely found new loves
and new employers when Daddy left for Cairo, she
kept to term his legacy, cherished or embarrassing.

When he came home to us at last, looked at me,
did he wonder if his other child likewise inherited
his freckles, Tartar nose, blue eyes, carrot hair?

Or did her mother's genes win out?

Years pass. Oceans apart, we've both
grown up, unknown to one another....
Did *she* in turn bear throwback progeny,
maintain his distant dynasty?

Or abandon them beyond the city gates
before they breathed the desert air,
shocked her tribe with unexpected
freckles, Tartar nose, carrot hair, blue eyes?

My sister, are you leading revolutions
or a herd of camels to the waterhole?

My Would-Be Siblings

*My father years later confided that I
was the only of several inconvenient
fetuses allowed to survive*

Small as Cornish hens, or quails,
bones fragile straws or supple
as cartilage of butterfly rays,

were you buried blessed,
a furtive interment after dark,
the stone left plain…? But where?

Or slipped into bins behind unmarked
back rooms, shutters drawn, then trucked
to local landfills with household trash?

To anonymous dumps for hospital detritus
beyond perimeters of foreign towns,
sent unsung to some fetal paradise?

Tiny ghosts whisper all night,
stir up specks of dust, or ash…
Do you conspire to materialize?

You are all here!
To claim your place by my side?
Or to nudge me aside?

VIII

Jorge Nikolaevich Artamonoff

Given Some Royal Hanky-Panky, Rather Illustrious Family Trees

Emails pour in with attachments and charts,
communiqués on and from our elegant dead
as if evites to virtual weddings:

Baron von This weds Baroness von That
who, to prolong the well-titled line,
bore baronettes like juvenile penguins
with multiple unpronounceable names.

We have not been invited to christenings yet
though these happened a century or two ago.

I was unsure if this story mere gossip:
Tsar Alex the First loved a lady-in-waiting,
the Court artist's beautiful daughter, noble but
not royal enough to become a tsarina.

Still, they engendered a child before the tsar
had to marry her off to a willing aristocrat,
a gentleman-in-waiting who bestowed his name
and, let us hope, his love for the lady
and the impending half-kingly baby.

Research now confirms what my father related.

And that royal engendering led in a few generations
to my own patrician cousin who confided,
"…in our line, several pairs of third
cousins fell in love with third cousins.
Only oceans kept *us* apart."
Meanwhile *his* progeny bear
those garnet drops of royal blood
albeit considerably watered down.

Re my future suitors, I'll consult Peerage,
and inquire about their blood types.

Notes for a Family Chronicle

1.

We were present and one
in one ancient drop
of semen briny as seas

Those rampant chromosomes
swords drawn, already wearing boots
thighs gripping saddles and loves

drove our brother-grandfathers
across mountains, rivers, steppes
caressing black earth, grey dust, beige manes

the blood of princes, tsars,
rushing to their heads
crying for blood, for milk

marching, wandering, returning
loyal, disillusioned, dying
alone

2.

And we, as isolate, unknown
and continents apart
ripped forth to light

drank light from fireflies
glow worms in the mud
stars

learned to give light
in weirdly mirrored hemisphere
in ignorance

fighting our fathers'
sensuality within ourselves
sometimes with success

Cold oceans and hot seas
divide our fates
but in our passport photographs

you wear my eyes
and I your wide
cheekbones and jaws

3.

Suddenly into my land-locked days
your tides break dikes
flow through

as I untangle and entangle you
in my wild currents
where honeysuckle whirls

We fear
and dare
maelstroms

Beneath the waves
the golden fish
still sing to us

Swim to me, sea beast
from one Devonian ocean
Together we'll crawl up the beach

You will teach me to walk on the earth
I will teach you to fly
Though apart, let us learn how to soar

across time zones, frontiers
We already know
our bones are as one

Feel the milk
of my breasts
in your veins

Taste the blood
from your wrists
on my nipples

Pharaohs in their specialized divinity
defying madness and taboos of common folk
married with their sisters

Place your hands on my Sheba belly
my Solomon, my brother
I am great with you

In here is where
antique and royal chromosomes
rejuvenate

link up, rebind and unify
those noble old alliances
and glorious coronations

4.

We burst with crowns of glow worms, fireflies, stars
and once again pass on
as one

Communiqués from an Émigré

1.

Have we faded from each other's lives the way
creased photographs fade, and people in wars
lose each other? Our fathers, second cousins,
lost contact through several wars…

2.

You were nine in Occupied Belgium when
without warning SS soldiers snatched your class
of blond blue-eyed sons of Old Russian exiles,
locked you onto an eastbound train to grow up
Aryan, become future janissaries for Germany.
They made you goosestep Berlin streets,
salute their swastikas, sing *Deutschland Uber Alles*,
aim a wooden rifle, triage wounded from the Front.

Allied planes hit their targets, rations grew sparse,
you learned to scavenge in the ruins of Cologne.

In Brussels, your parents mourned a kidnapped child.
Your mother descended from Nicholas I (product
of his love for the court artist's daughter noble yet
a tsar must marry a full-blooded princess, albeit imported).

Do royalty, legitimacy, bereavement, matter to soldiers,
bare cupboards, soup kitchens, bombs? One carries on.

3.

World War Two through, your father, now head of
a UN refugee camp, retrieved you. My father located
yours, helped you all launch new lives in Brazil.
Did you relearn a childhood in peace? You studied
languages, engineering and Buddhism, prospered,
married, spoke seldom of war, not to your children…

4.

We met in warm South Atlantic surf. You, *distingué*
as a prince, resembled my dashing father.
The same books lined your shelves as lined mine,
our children born the same years looked like siblings.
We both had suitable spouses. Neither remained forever.

5.

Your rare visits north, you held my hand on the street—
normal in Latin lands, but in North America then reserved
for sweethearts, genuine fiancés. We never became
bona fide lovers. Still, you left footprints on my poems…

6.

Thirty years later, hemispheres apart, we wrote
every day, emailed on the Internet, and shared
histories, secrets, quotidian details, first drafts.
Like twins or lovers, we thought the same thoughts
the same moment, learned we'd cooked the same meals,
suffered similar ailments, each cared for a damaged son.
Ancestral ghosts wandered into our lives without notice.

At last you described your dangerous childhood.
Your letters showed me how to survive, how to live.
Dangers persist, wait to catch us off guard…

7.

Without warning you have cut the connection,
our daily tryst in the stratosphere. No news, no obit,
no one down there thinks to write, or knows where.
To whom could I write? For whom?

8.

Today I learn: *you are alive*!
So, we will both die old, far apart
but, perhaps, both on the same night…

9.

Silenced, now I mourn, and cannot accept
that you died without first telling me.

IX

Elspeth Cameron Ritchie, Alexander George Ritchie, Lyell Kirk Ritchie
Washington, DC 1965

Your Crazy Pumpkin Vine

That vine is racing three-fourths of the way
around your yard's circumference—
yard, not garden, a mere scruffy plot
of grass and moss, but *yours*.
The verb *to race* expresses speed
relative in the vegetable kingdom.

One seed survived from Halloween's
sunken pumpkin tossed in the compost heap
with leaves you raked and grass you mowed
in your late-blooming flurry of conformity
to these suburban neighborhoods
spurned through your rebellious youth.

You too struck out alone, and raced
round the globe, then, to square a circle,
turned, came mostly home.

These tendrils clutch your anchor fence
yet don't climb too high, might sense
nascent fruit would swell and weigh enough
to pull pumpkins, vine and fence to earth.

Buds blossom in whatever patch of sun then,
like you, in time bear sumptuous progeny.

My Daughter Borrows Two Eggs

To feed her new lover
oeuf a` la coque
with a rose in its mouth...

At a long-ago breakfast
my father explained to *my* lover
the symbolism of eggs:

"Fertility, hope, and perfection.
In oval domes atop Russian churches
the Holy Trinity rolled into one."

What if, when the bells ring so hard
at midnight on Easter,
gold cupolas hatched into mystical roosters...

My father, ill and en route
to that perfect elliptical void,
has trouble spooning his morning egg.

Yet how much he could tell
of the liquid ovoid of loving,
fragile shells.

Still, today he bequeaths
to his waiting granddaughter:
perfection, fertility, hope,

a remembered triad embedded
in two speckled X-Large eggs
with golden yolks.

Hibiscus Child, Born on Cyprus

Hibiscus hedges crimson and salmon
encircled your birth on that hot
island where copper surf beat copper
rocks, turquoise waves curled ephemeral
as petals you grasped in miniature hands.

Midwives in snow-white gowns
like a ring of fairy godmothers
promised you beauty and brilliance.
They forgot to mention fortune, fame,
safe journeys, or common sense.

Slighted by your beneficent witches,
still you blossomed...But now
you charge about on perennial quests,
scatter copper and gold to strangers,
fickle bouquets to every girl,

while we stand by confused:
your trails of promises broken,
unpayable debts, and pain...

Far from you now in a snowy land,
I watch the hibiscus plant on my sill
swell into flowers, one every day.
Each lasts only a day. That flashy cycle
completed, rooted in silence again
the plant retreats into green,
like you changing mood with the season,
thirst never slaked, storing blooms
complex and red as our shared blood...

Yuri/George Leonidovich Artamonoff,
Alexander George Ritchie, Beirut 1964

X

On The Red Arrow Express

Moscow to Leningrad 1988

Imagine if I had been born among birches
and barricades, gold domes and gulags,
in this dangerous land, familiar and strange
from childhood, first seen now in a luminous

Arctic July...Whom would I have loved?
Would you have appeared on this train
at this hour, would we have known
how to speak with each other?

Would my hedonistic rebellious nature
be tempered by merciless winters,
unseasonal famines, eternal threats
of prison and wars?

In a 1942 photograph of the Siege
women are digging an anti-tank trench
or a mass grave. One girl lifts a spade
heavy with rubble, smiles at the camera.

Cheekbones wide, eyes too close, untidy curls.
Rib-thin. My double, age ten. A cousin?
Did she survive the Blockade? Would I have?
The train rockets on between cabbage fields...

A Different Wine-Dark Sea, Moscow, 1986

"Summer not my time to write,"
our hostess shrugs, and obliges guests
with smoky tea, Armenian cognac,
her old poem about Homer.

The table glows with apricots,
glistens with gooseberry jam.
Curls of chocolate feather
the gift of an almond torte.

Then from her broken balcony:
a colder breeze invades.
A turned leaf blows across the floor
like a scrap, or a word.

Suddenly she lines her books like troops,
rakes wrinkled pages from a drawer.
Guests exchange glances, rise.
She does not detain them with chatter.

On his stormy wine dark sea
Homer could not know
such brutal change of season.
Homer did not fear

a black car stopped by the gate,
or men in gray overcoats
entering the courtyard. At times
we must all become blind.

Djigit, You Trick Rider

Be careful, tight-rope walker on wind,
on spider strands stretched from white peaks,
can you keep your footing above the abyss?

They dangle gold coins…Will you stretch
from your saddle to snatch with your teeth
the silver kinjal thrust in the ground?

You gallop so fast you will fall,
bruise your lips on the stones
mix your hot blood with the dust—

Wind unfurls your wild hair, your mare's mane,
erases her hoof prints, your blood—But not the love
which drives you to revolt against fate…

Correspondence with a Russian Sailor

What a decade of letters I've sent
to Piraeus, Naples, Hong Kong, Istanbul,
Singapore, Panama, Havre, Bombay,

an atlas of foreign ports
fragrant with cinnamon, seaweed,
petroleum, coal dust, fish.

Your ship lands, you rush down the gangplank –
Guards challenge your passport.
Vendors, taverns, girls intercept.

At last you find the POSTE RESTANTE window –
Surabaya, Yokohama, Rio, Marseilles –
"No mail for this name? Look again..."

You post your flimsy envelopes stamped
with vermilion fishes, indigo moths,
portraits of local heroes.

Our letters get lost between salutation
and dock. Still we write until lines
scrawled on pages etch in our faces.

We scribble on water, on fog,
the shoulders of dolphins,
hummingbird feathers, cicada wings.

Danger needs no spelling out.
When one rare note arrives,
sentences catch in the screech

of cables round winches, words rush
with hawsers through chocks,
tear in the din of derricks and bells.

Gulls mistake flutters of shredded letters
for bread. Kisses XXX-ed in black ink
trickle like precious fresh water

into the languorous suck of salt waves
around pilings and hulls, while tide
lowers tons of metal and men

toward the muck of the harbor floor,
layers of sunken ships, driftwood, tires,
shells, exoskeletons, bones.

Amid jetsam of ocean and land
meanings hide, you disappear...
And still we write.

"Alaska Wild Berries," courtesy of U.S. Fish & Wildlife Service

Wild Berries

Another famine in a land
where curious watchers betray,
a lover told me how he set off
alone to gather berries in his pail.

He picked and picked, then,
surprised by snuffles from the far
side of the berry patch, called out,
"But who is weeping there?"

No answer, so he stepped around
screening vines like barbed wire,
all of a sudden nose to nose
with a large brown bear.

They stared, then each backed away.
The bear had slaked his lust for fruit,
the hungry lover abandoned his
heavy pail amid the briars.

He recounted this to me while,
in a safer clime, we slipped
from spying eyes to thorny vines.
Juice dyed our faces, hands, and clothes.

Mid purpled kisses, we remained aware
what dangers wait beyond the woods,
how stolen berries are indeed more sweet,
how indelible the stains.

Photograph in Black-and-White

Oaks hunch black
above the farmhouse   white
we borrowed last night

The black door locks
night's warmth inside
our stolen night

You stand beside
gray hollyhocks
beyond gray lawn

your striped shirt wrinkles gray
eyelids wrinkle gray
gray fists clench tight

before your homeward flight
to that dark land
where only snow is white

Gray lips unsmiling clamp
in all you must not speak
I must not write

      Or write with wax on a handkerchief
      fashion a frame to contain
      all that grief

      Words beneath the wax
      in a cauldron come to light
      all unwritten will not

How can shapes and blots
of lives steaming with pain
and so much love be forgot

My camera trembles not
from chill of gray
first light

A Dream of Death in Siberia

The death occurs
in one of those hamlets,
refuge of hermits and Doukhobors,

where the single path in
was masked by lichen and moss
centuries ago.

A stranger stops
for one night in a hut,
gives no name...

Snow flecked with red
begins to melt
over the frozen mud.

Flies and mosquitoes wait
under puddles of ice
to wing through leached air

when the tundra explodes
in purple and yellow anemones.
Now the earth remains stone.

So the deceased
lies in the shed,
cannot be planted yet.

He leaves an unstrung guitar,
a patched coat, boots with holes,
a linen shirt with a monogram

no one can decipher. The lines
on his palms predicted
betrayal and danger,

broken stitches told wandering,
the curve of his arc—
a reader of dreams.

No-Shows

I wanted all of you *live*.
Why did some die
en route to the party?
The best even fell
before leaving home.

Others, long dead, crept
through garden windows,
the kitchen door, half drunk
bottles in hand, years late.

What can I offer now?
Flat beer, vinegar-wine,
anemic champagne?

Cockatoos finished the caviar,
roaches the camembert,
mice left trails on the plates.

True, we've all changed.
New lines etch our palms.
Will we have voices to sing,
an audience to applaud?

Yet we agreed to greet
the New Year together again.
The table is set.
My blackberry vodka is chilled.

I'll expect you at ten.

Acknowledgments

"Abdication:" *Washingtonian Magazine* 1976; *Moving To Larger Quarters*, Artists' and Writers' Collaborative, Manila, ©1977 Elisavietta Ritchie;

"Aunt Maria Leonidovna Tells Me Her War Stories over Tea:" *Tiger Upstairs on Connecticut Avenue,* Cherry Grove Collections, WordTech Communications, © 2013 Elisavietta Ritchie;

"The Ancestors Wait, Wet:" *Lalitamba* 2016; *Prosopisia,* anthology editor Anuraag Sharma, 2016;

"Babushka's Beads:" ©2007 by Elisavietta Ritchie; *Potomac Review* 2007; *Canadian Woman Studies,* 2007; *Cormorant beyond the Compost,* Cherry Grove Collections, WordTech Communications, ©2011 Elisavietta Ritchie;

"Blood Lines" (excerpt): *Guy Wires,* Poets' Choice Publishing, ©2105 Elisavietta Ritchie;

"Communiqués from an Émigré:" *Tiger Upstairs on Connecticut Avenue,* Cherry Grove Collections, WordTech Communications ©2013 Elisavietta Ritchie;

"Correspondence with a Russian Sailor:" *Cincinnati Poetry Review; The Arc of the Storm,* Signal Books, ©1998 Elisavietta Ritchie;

"Djigit:" *Tightening The Circle Over Eel Country*, Acropolis Books, ©1974 Elisavietta Ritchie, (won Great Lakes Colleges Association's "New Writer's Award for Best First Book of Poetry," 1975-1976);

"A Dream of Death in Siberia:" *Gypsy,* (journal won 1989 Amnesty International Award)*; A Wound-Up Cat & Other Bedtime Stories,* Palmerston Press, ©1993 Elisavietta Ritchie*; The Arc of the Storm,* Signal Books, ©1998 Elisavietta Ritchie;

"Family Ghosts:" *Cincinnati Poetry Review*, 1995; *The Arc of the Storm,* Signal Books, ©1998 Elisavietta Ritchie;

"Flying Time:" *Home Planet News; A Wound-Up Cat and Other Bedtime Stories,* Palmerston Press, ©1993 Elisavietta Ritchie*; Grow Old Along With Me, The Best Is Yet To Be,* Sandra Martz, editor, Papier Mache Press, 1996; *The Arc of the Storm,* Signal Books, ©1998 Elisavietta Ritchie; in story "Flying Time," winner 1986 PEN Syndicated Fiction competition, in *Flying Time: Stories & Half-Stories* Signal Books, ©1992 &1996 Elisavietta Ritchie;

"A Geography of Genes:" *Island (*Tasmania) 1997; *Ascent* 1999; *Awaiting Permission to Land,* Cherry Grove Collections, WordTech Communications, ©2006 Elisavietta Ritchie;

"Given Some Royal Hanky-Panky, Rather Illustrious Family Trees:" as "On Illustrious Ancestors:" *Guy Wires,* Poets' Choice Publishing, ©2105 Elisavietta Ritchie;

"Great Aunt Eugenya's Mattress:" *Inkwell,* December 1998;

"Guest of Honor:" ©1974 *New York Times; Tightening The Circle Over Eel Country,* Acropolis Books, ©1974 Elisavietta Ritchie, (won Great Lakes Colleges Association's "New Writer's Award for Best First Book of Poetry," 1975-1976);

"Halvah, Toronto:" ©1995 *The Christian Science Monitor; Potomac Review,* 2005; *Awaiting Permission to Land,* (won Anamnesis Manuscript Award), Cherry Grove Collections, WordTech Communications, ©2006 Elisavietta Ritchie;

"Hibiscus Child:" *Kairos,* 1994; *The Arc of the Storm,* Signal Books, ©1998 Elisavietta Ritchie;

"Improvements:" *Canto; Raking The Snow, (*won Washington Writers' Publishing House 1981 competition), ©1982 Elisavietta Ritchie;

"Snow in Leningrad:" *muse-apprentice-guild website* summer 2004; *Potomac Review* 2005; *Hello, Goodbye: Stories, Essays and Poems for the Twenty-First Century,* ©2004, anthology editor, Gay Baines, July Literary Press; *Awaiting Permission to Land* (won Anamnesis Manuscript Award), Cherry Grove Collections, Word-Tech Communications, ©2006 Elisavietta Ritchie;

"Teatime with Babushka, Age Ninety-Four:" *Tightening The Circle Over Eel Country,* Acropolis Books, ©1974 Elisavietta Ritchie, (won Great Lakes Colleges Association's "New Writer's Award for Best First Book of Poetry," 1975-1976);

"Thanksgiving with Great Aunt Eugenya:" *The Ledge,* 2000; *Awaiting Permission to Land* (won Anamnesis Manuscript Award), Cherry Grove Collections, WordTech Communications, ©2006 Elisavietta Ritchie;

"Visiting Great Aunt Eugenya by the Chesapeake:" *The American Scholar,* ©1996 The Phi Beta Kappa Society; *The Arc of the Storm,* Signal Books, ©1998 Elisavietta Ritchie;

"Visiting Rites:" *A Sheath of Dreams & Other Games,* Proteus Press, ©1976 Elisavietta Ritchie;

"While It Rains:" *Potomac Review,* Fall 2005; *Awaiting Permission To Land* (won Anamnesis Manuscript Award); Cherry Grove Collections, WordTech Communications, ©2006 Elisavietta Ritchie;

"While Our Fathers Are Dying:" *Inkwell,* 2002; *Awaiting Permission to Land* (won Anamnesis Manuscript Award) Cherry Grove Collections, WordTech Communications, ©2006 Elisavietta Ritchie;

"The Wine-Dark Sea:" *Cincinnati Poetry Review; The Arc of the Storm,* Signal Books, ©1998 Elisavietta Ritchie;

"Your Crazy Pumpkin Vine:" prose version ©2000 *The Christian Science Monitor; The Arc of the Storm,* Signal Books, ©1998 Elisavietta Ritchie.

About the Author

Elisavietta Ritchie's poetry, fiction, creative non-fiction, translations and photojournalism are widely published, anthologized and translated. *Guy Wires* (Poets' Choice Publishing) was the latest of over seventeen collections. A revised edition of *In Haste I Write You This Note: Stories & Half-Stories* became an e-book (Washington Writers' Publishing House), both in 2015.

Raking the Snow a winner of the collaborative Washington Writers' Publishing House in 1981, she served for three years as president for poetry. When *In Haste I Write You This Note: Stories & Half Stories* won the WWPH premiere fiction award in 1999, because nobody else was available then, she became co-president of the fiction division for a decade. She remains as an editor.

Flying Time: Stories & Half-Stories her first fiction collection, a third is in progress. Other full poetry collections include *Tiger Upstairs on Connecticut Avenue; Feathers, Or, Love on the Wing; Cormorant Beyond the Compost; Awaiting Permission to Land; The Arc of the Storm; Elegy for the Other Woman,* and *Tightening The Circle Over Eel Country* which won the Great Lakes Colleges Association's "New Writer's Award, 1975-1976." Individual poems and stories won awards, and several were nominated for the Pushcart Prize. Among her literary translations are Aleksandr Blok's *The Twelve,* Anna Akhmatova's early and late love poems, and Lyubov Sirota's *Chernobyl* sequence.

After attending the Sorbonne and Cornell, Ritchie received her BA from Berkeley, her MA as a graduate teaching fellow at American University. In the 1970s the United States Information Service sent her around Brazil, the Far East, and the Balkans as a "Visiting American Poet" to give readings and meet with fellow writers.

Ritchie serves as poet-in-the-schools and mentor to fellow writers in Washington DC, Maryland and beyond. At Calvert Library, in Prince Frederick, Maryland she created on-going workshops in poetry, memoir and creative writing. Her articles, poetry, creative non-fiction and photographs appeared in *The New York Times, Christian Science Monitor, National Geographic* and many literary publications. Currently she freelances as a photojournalist for *The Bay Weekly.*

With poet Myra Sklarew she founded A Splendid Wake to honor over a century of departed poets who lived and wrote in the Greater Washington Area, and this organization now counts hundreds of participants.

After assignments in Europe, the United States, Canada and Australia, Ritchie and her writer husband Clyde Farnsworth, formerly a *New York Times* reporter, now live and write in Washington DC and beside the Patuxent River in Southern Maryland.

A Note on the Gallery of Artists

In a serendipitous moment for poetry and art, we attended a poetry reading where Christopher Passehl, the husband of the featured poet, Janet Passehl, designed the cover to his wife's book. Passehl teaches the extremely talented students from the Advanced Graphic Design course at the University of New Haven. We created a project in which his students tried their hand at a cover for *BABUSHKA'S BEADS*, letting the author choose the "winner." Each student had a different take on the poems, some stressing Russian themes, others focusing on the ancient clock which inspired the poems. All were so interesting we decided to include them all by way of thanking the student designers for their work and letting readers meet these up and coming talents. We salute them with gratitude for the work found at the end of this manuscript: Sal d'Angelo (Cover), Zelenia Echevarria, Antoinette Canieso, Marzi Esfandiari, Jalisa Johnson, Gloria Blount and Sade King.

BABUSKA'S BEADS:

A GEOGRAPHY OF GENES

NEW AND REVISED SELECTED POEMS OF
RUSSIAN LINEAGE

*E*LISAVIETTA *R*ITCHIE

by Sade King

BABUSHKA'S BEADS:
A GEOGRAPHY OF GENES

New and Revised Selected Poems
of Russian Lineage

Elisavietta Ritchie

by Zelenia Echevarria

Babushka's Beads:

A GEOGRAPHY OF GENES

New and Revised Selected Poems
of Russian Lineage

Elisavietta Ritchie

by Antoinette Canieso

Babushka's Beads

A Geography of Genes

New and revised selected poems

of Russian lineage

Elisavietta Ritchie

by Marzi Esfandiari

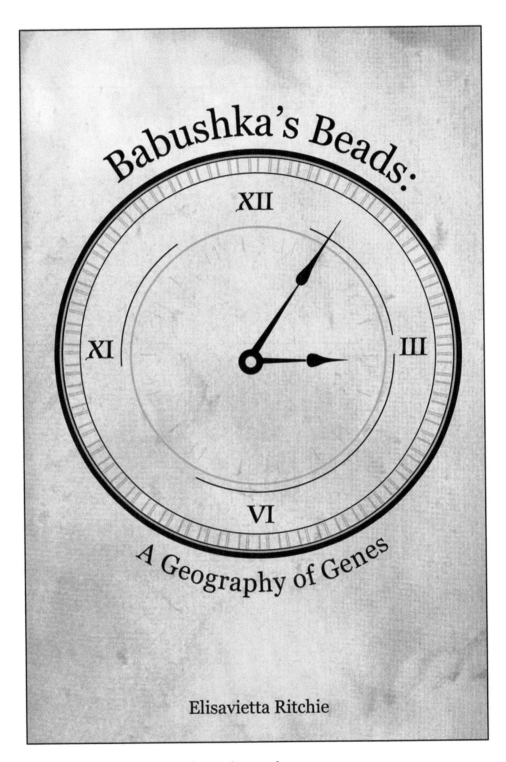

Babushka's Beads:

A Geography of Genes

Elisavietta Ritchie

by Jalisa Johnson

BABUSHKA'S BEADS:

A GEOGRAPHY OF GENES

NEW AND REVISED SELECTED POEMS OF RUSSIAN LINEAGE

ELISAVIETTA RITCHIE

by Gloria Blount

List of Illustrations

CPSIA information can be obtained
at www.ICGtesting.com
Printed in the USA
LVOW01s1626210416
484698LV00048B/300/P